Pennsylvania Dutch Cooking

IN 1683 the Plain Sects began to arrive in William Penn's Colony seeking a land of peace and plenty. They were a mixed people; Moravians from Bohemia and Moravia, Mennonites from Switzerland and Holland, the Amish, the Dunkards, the Schwenkfelds, and the French Huguenots. After the lean years of clearing the land and developing their farms they established the peace and plenty they sought. These German-speaking people were originally called the Pennsylvania Deutsch but time and custom have caused them to be known to us as the Pennsylvania Dutch.

The Pennsylvania Dutch are a hard working people and as they say, "Them that works hard, eats hearty." The blending of recipes from their many home lands and the ingredients available in their new land produced tasty dishes that have been handed down from mother to daughter for generations. Their cooking was truly a folk art requiring much intuitive knowledge, for recipes contained measurements such as "flour to stiffen," "butter the size of a walnut," and "large as an apple." Many of the recipes have been made more exact and standardized providing us with a regional cookery we can all enjoy.

Soups are a traditional part of Pennsylvania Dutch cooking and the Dutch housewife can apparently make soup out of anything. If she has only milk and flour she can still make rivel soup. However, most of their soups are sturdier dishes, hearty enough to serve as the major portion of the evening meal. One of the favorite summer soups in the Pennsylvania Dutch country is Chicken Corn Soup. Few Sunday School picnic suppers would be considered complete without gallons of this hearty soup.

Many of the Pennsylvania Dutch foods are a part of their folklore. No Shrove Tuesday would be complete without raised doughnuts called "fastnachts." One of the many folk tales traces this custom back to the burnt offerings made by their old country ancestors to the goddess of spring. With the coming of Christianity the custom became associated with the Easter season and "fastnachts" are eaten on Shrove Tuesday to insure living to next Shrove Tuesday. Young dandelion greens are eaten on Maundy Thursday in order to remain well throughout the year.

The Christmas season is one of the busiest times in the Pennsylvania Dutch kitchen. For weeks before Christmas the house is filled with the smell of almond cookies, anise cookies, sandtarts,

Belsnickle Christmas cookies, walnut kisses, pfeffernusse, and other traditional cookies. Not just a few of one kind but dozens and dozens of many kinds of cookies must be made. There must be plenty for the enjoyment of the family and many holiday visitors.

Regardless of the time of the year or the time of the day there are pies. The Pennsylvania Dutch eat pies for breakfast. They eat pies for lunch. They eat pies for dinner and they eat pies for midnight snacks. Pies are made with a great variety of ingredients from the apple pie we all know to the rivel pie which is made from flour, sugar, and butter. The Dutch housewife is as generous with her pies as she is with all her cooking, baking six or eight at a time not one and two.

The apple is an important Pennsylvania Dutch food. Dried apples form the basis for many typical dishes. Each fall barrels of apples are converted into cider. Apple butter is one of the Pennsylvania Dutch foods which has found national acceptance. The making of apple butter is an all-day affair and has the air of a holiday to it. Early in the morning the neighbors gather and begin to peel huge piles of apples that will be needed. Soon the great copper apple butter kettle is brought out and set up over a wood fire. Apple butter requires constant stirring to prevent burning. However, stirring can be light work for a boy and a girl when they're young and the day is bright and the world is full of promise. By dusk the apple butter is made, neighborhood news is brought up to date and hunger has been driven that much further away for the coming winter.

Food is abundant and appetites are hearty in the Pennsylvania Dutch country. The traditional dishes are relatively simple and unlike most regional cookery the ingredients are readily available. Best of all, no matter who makes them the results are "wonderful good."

PENNSYLVANIA DUTCH

Salads

FRUIT SALAD DRESSING

- **½ cup sugar**
- **1½ tblsp. flour**
- **2 eggs**
- **½ cup pineapple juice**
- **½ cup lemon juice**
- **1 cup whipped cream**

Combine the fruit juices and stir slowly into the flour and sugar. Cook. Stirring constantly, until it thickens. (or cook in double boiler) Add the beaten eggs and cook for another minute. Let cool and fold in the whipped cream.

BEET *AND* APPLE SALAD

- **2 cups apples, diced**
- **2 cups cooked beets, diced**
- **¼ cup chopped nuts**

- **2 hard boiled eggs**
- **½ cup salad dressing**
- **parsley**

Mix the apples, beets, and chopped eggs. Add salad dressing (see Grandma's salad dressing). Mix and garnish with chopped nuts and parsley.

A GOOD PENNSYLVANIA DUTCH SALAD DRESSING

- **2 hard boiled eggs, mashed**
- **a little grated onion**
- **3 tablespoons salad oil**
- **1 tablespoon vinegar**
- **½ teaspoon salt**
- **pinch of pepper**

Mix well together, then put on lettuce and turn and stir until it is well covered with the dressing. Good with any green salad.

PEPPER CABBAGE

- **2 cups shredded cabbage**
- **1 large green pepper**
- **½ cup hot salad dressing**
- **1 tsp. salt**

Mix the cabbage, pepper, chopped fine and salt. Let stand 1 hour in cool place. Drain off all liquid. Make a hot dressing with:

- **1 tblsp. butter**
- **1 tsp. flour**
- **½ tsp. dry mustard**
- **salt and pepper**
- **yolk of 1 egg**
- **½ cup vinegar**

Melt the butter and blend in the flour. Add vinegar and stir until mixture thickens. Mix mustard, salt and pepper and add to the liquid. Cool for 4 minutes, pour over the beaten egg yolk and mix well. Cook for 1 minute more. Pour this over the pepper cabbage and mix well.

POTATO SALAD DRESSING

- **1 beaten egg**
- **½ cup sugar**
- **1 tbsp. flour**
- **½ cup water**
- **½ cup vinegar**
- **2 tbsp. butter**
- **½ tsp. salt**
- **¼ tsp. pepper**

Combine in the order given, stirring after each addition. Boil until thick. Cool before adding to the salad.

BEAN SALAD

- **3 cups navy beans baked or boiled**
- **1 medium onion**
- **2 tblsp. pickle relish or 1-large pickle**
- **3 hard boiled eggs**
- **2 tblsp. vinegar**
- **⅔ cup boiled salad dressing**
- **1½ tsp. salt**

Chop the onion fine, the boiled eggs, add the relish, or the pickle, chopped and the beans. Mix well together and add salt and salad dressing. Chill and serve. Green string beans, cut in 1-inch pieces may be used for this salad.

DANDELION SALAD

- **Young dandelion greens**
- **4 thick slices bacon**
- **½ cup cream**
- **2 tblsp. butter**
- **2 eggs**
- **1 tsp. salt**
- **1 tblsp. sugar**
- **4 tblsp. vinegar**
- **½ tsp. paprika**
- **black pepper**

Wash dandelions and pick over carefully. Roll in cloth and pat dry. Put into a salad bowl and set in warm place. Cut bacon in small cubes, fry quickly and pour over dandelions. Put butter and cream into a skillet and melt over low heat. Beat eggs, add salt, pepper, sugar and vinegar, then mix with the slightly warm cream mixture. Cook over high heat until dressing is quite thick. Pour, very hot, over the dandelions, stir well and serve.

PENNSYLVANIA COLE SLAW

- **1 head young cabbage**
- **½ cup cream**
- **1 teaspoon salt**
- **½ cup sugar**
- **½ cup vinegar**

Beat cream, sugar, vinegar and salt together thoroughly until the dressing is like whipped cream. Discard outer leaves of cabbage. Shred the rest finely and combine with dressing just before it is ready to serve. Serves six. As variation: Add shredded green and red peppers.

DEVILED EGGS

- **6 hard-boiled eggs**
- **½ tsp. prepared mustard**
- **2 tsp. soft butter**
- **salt, pepper, paprika**

Remove shells and cut eggs in half. Mash the yolks to a smooth paste, adding the mustard, butter, salt and pepper. When well mixed press into the cup-shaped egg whites, round the tops and sprinkle with paprika. For a special treat, add 2 tblsp. finely chopped ham or a small can of deviled ham to the egg yolk mixture.

HOT DUTCH POTATO SALAD

- **4 slices bacon**
- **½ cup chopped onion**
- **½ cup chopped green pepper**
- **¼ cup vinegar**
- **1 teaspoon salt**
- **3 hard boiled eggs**
- **⅛ teaspoon pepper**
- **1 teaspoon sugar**
- **1 egg**

- **1 qt. hot, cubed, cooked potatoes**
- **¼ cup grated raw carrot**

Dice bacon and pan fry. Add chopped onion and green pepper. Cook 3 minutes. Add vinegar, salt, pepper, sugar and beaten egg. Cook slightly. Add cubed potatoes, grated carrot and diced hard-cooked eggs. Blend and serve hot.

HOT SLAW

Shred cabbage finely. Boil in slightly salted water until tender. Drain. Serve hot thoroughly mixed with warm cooked salad dressing made as follows:

- **½ teaspoon mustard**
- **1½ teaspoons salt**
- **1½ teaspoons sugar**
- **1½ tablespoons flour**
- **⅛ teaspoon pepper**
- **1 beaten egg**
- **1 cup milk**
- **4 tablespoons vinegar**
- **1½ tablespoons butter**

Mix mustard, salt, sugar, flour, paprika and pepper. Add egg and mix thoroughly. Add milk and vinegar. Cook over hot water, stirring frequently until thick. Add butter. Cook and stir until melted.

CUCUMBER SALAD

- **2 medium cucumbers**
- **1 medium onion**
- **salt**
- **2 tblsp. vinegar**
- **sour cream**
- **pepper**

Pare and thinly slice cucumber and onion sprinkle with a teaspoon of salt and let stand for a few minutes. Pat with towel or absorbent paper to take out all moisture possible. Place cucumbers and onions in serving dish, add the vinegar and mix. Pour on enough sour cream to half cover and dust with pepper. Chill.

PENNSYLVANIA DUTCH

Soups

PHILADELPHIA PEPPER POT

- **1 lb. honeycomb tripe**
- **1 veal knuckle**
- **1½ qts. water**
- **2 tablespoons salt**
- **1 tblsp. red pepper, diced**
- **1 tblsp. green pepper, diced**
- **1 tablespoon powdered thyme**
- **6 peppercorns**
- **4 potatoes, diced**
- **2 bay leaves**
- **3 whole cloves**
- **3 tablespoons chopped parsley**
- **2 stalks celery, diced**
- **2 carrots, diced**
- **2 tomatoes, peeled, cut up**
- **4 onions, thinly sliced**
- **1 piece pimento, cut fine**

Wash and scrub tripe thoroughly. Place in large kettle and cover with plenty of cold water. Bring to a boil and simmer until tender. Simmer without boiling, that is the secret of making tripe tender. Drain and dice, ½ inch squares. In the meantime place the veal knuckle in another kettle adding 1½ qts. of water and all ingredients except the potatoes. Simmer at least one hour, put in potatoes and simmer for another hour or until meat falls off the bone. Remove bone and take off all the meat. Cut it into small pieces and together with the tripe put it back into the soup. Bring to a boil and the soup is ready to serve. This soup keeps well and can be reheated.

DUMPLINGS (Spaetzle)

- **1 cup milk**
- **2 cups flour**
- **2 eggs**
- **1 tsp. salt**

Add milk to flour slowly, stirring constantly to keep mixture smooth. Add 1 egg at a time, beating well after each addition. Salt and mix well. When cooking in boiling salted water or meat broth, pour the batter from a shallow bowl, tilting it over the boiling kettle. With a sharp knife slice off pieces of the batter into the boiling liquid. Dip knife in the liquid before each cut to prevent sticking.

CORN CHOWDER

- **4 slices bacon**
- **2 tblsp. onion, minced**
- **1 tblsp. celery, minced**
- **1 tblsp. pepper, minced**
- **2 cups corn**
- **2 potatoes, diced**
- **3 tomatoes, cut-up**
- **2 pints milk**
- **salt**
- **pepper**

Dice the bacon and put into pan to brown, add onion, celery and pepper; fry until bacon is crisp. Add the corn and saute together for 3 minutes. Add the potatoes, tomatoes and seasoning, cover and simmer for 30 minutes. Finally add the milk, heat to the boiling point and serve with a little chopped parsley.

EGG NOODLES

- **2 eggs**
- **½ tsp. salt**
- **sifted flour**

Add salt to the eggs and work in enough flour to make a stiff dough. Knead thoroughly, divide into 2 portions and roll each out as thin as possible, on a floured board. Cover with cloth and let stand until partly dry. Roll up the dough and cut into ¼ inch strips. Spread out on paper to dry a little longer.

DUTCH COUNTRY BEAN SOUP

- **1 lb. soup beans**
- **1 ham bone**
- **½ cup chopped onion**
- **1 cup diced celery**
- **1 can tomato sauce**
- **½ cup diced potatoes**
- **2 tsp. minced parsley**
- **salt and pepper**

Soak beans in water overnight. Drain, add fresh water and cook slowly with the ham bone for 2 hours. Put in the onion, celery, potatoes, tomato sauce, parsley and the salt and pepper and simmer until vegetables are soft. Remove the ham bone, trim off any meat, cut it up and add to soup. Many Pennsylvania Dutch cooks cut up hard boiled eggs and add them to the soup.

SPLIT PEA SOUP

- **1 lb. split peas**
- **3 qts. water**
- **1 ham bone**
- **salt**
- **2 carrots, sliced**
- **1 stalk celery, chopped**
- **1 large onion, chopped**
- **pepper**

Wash peas, add cold water, vegetables and ham bone and simmer for three hours or until mixture is thick. Remove ham bone, force peas through coarse sieve and season to taste. Dilute with milk. Serve with toasted croutons.

VEGETABLE SOUP

- **1 soup bone**
- **2 lbs. stewing beef**
- **2 qts. water**
- **1 cup chopped onion**
- **1 cup chopped celery**
- **1 cup tomatoes**
- **2 tsp. salt**
- **black pepper**

Into 2 qts. of water put soup bone and beef and boil for 2 hours. For a hearty, substantial soup, cut up the meat in small pieces and return to the broth. Add tomatoes, onions and celery. Also add other available vegetables, such as diced potatoes, carrots, turnip, string beans, corn, peas, cabbage or chopped peppers. Boil until all vegetables are tender.

MEAT FILLING *FOR* NOODLES

- **1 cup ground beef**
- **2 tblsp. fat**
- **1 small onion**
- **½ cup dry bread crumbs**
- **1 cup bread cubes**
- **salt and pepper**
- **2 tblsp. butter**

Make a recipe of noodle dough (see above). Roll thin, let dry and cut into 3 inch squares. Brown meat in hot fat with the onion and seasoning. Soak bread cubes in water and press dry then add to the meat. Spoon mixture on the center of the noodle squares, fold in half and seal edges, like little pillows. Drop the filled squares into salted boiling water and cook 8 to 10 minutes. Lift carefully with draining spoon to a serving dish and top with the half cup of bread crumbs which have been browned in butter.

EGG BALLS FOR SOUP

Rub the yolks of three or four hard boiled eggs to a smooth paste and salt. To these add two raw ones lightly beaten. Add enough flour to hold the paste together. Make into balls with floured hands and set in cool place until just before your soup comes off. Put the balls carefully into the soup and boil one minute.

SPINACH FILLING *FOR* NOODLES

- **2 lbs. raw spinach, chopped**
- **3 tblsp. butter**
- **salt and pepper**
- **1½ cups bread crumbs**
- **2 eggs**

Make a recipe of noodle dough (see above). Steam and brown the spinach in melted butter. Add the eggs, 1 cup of dry bread crumbs and the seasoning. Mix well, spoon mixture on noodle dough squares and proceed as above.

SALSIFY *OR* VEGETABLE OYSTER SOUP

- **1½ cups diced salsify**
- **1½ cups water**
- **1 tblsp. vinegar**
- **1 tblsp. butter**
- **1 quart milk**
- **salt and pepper**

Scrub, scrape and clean salsify. Dice and cook in salted water, with 1 tablespoon of vinegar added, until tender. Drain, add butter and rich milk, salt and pepper. Bring to a boil and serve with crackers.

BEEF SOUP *WITH* DUMPLINGS

- **1 soup bone**
- **2 lbs. stewing beef**
- **2 quarts water**
- **salt**
- **1½ cups flour**
- **1 egg**
- **½ cup milk**
- **pepper**

Cook meat until tender and remove from the broth. Add water until you have 2 quarts of broth. Make dumplings by mixing beaten egg and milk into flour until about the consistency of pancake batter. Drop from teaspoon into the boiling broth to form small dumplings. Cook for 3 or 4 minutes.

POTATO SOUP (Gruumbier Suupe)

- **4 cups diced potatoes**
- **1 medium onion**
- **3 tblsp. flour**
- **1 tblsp. butter**
- **1 qt. milk**
- **1 egg, beaten**
- **salt and pepper**
- **parsley**

Boil potatoes and onion in small amount of water until soft. Add milk, salt and pepper then reheat. Brown flour in the butter and blend it slowly into the potato mixture. Add a little water to the beaten egg and stir into the soup. Let it cook for a few minutes and serve with a sprinkling of chopped parsley.

CHICKEN CORN SOUP

- **1 stewing hen, about 4-lbs.**
- **4 qts. water**
- **1 onion, chopped**
- **10 ears corn**
- **½ cup celery, chopped with leaves**
- **2 hard-boiled eggs**
- **salt and pepper**
- **rivels**

Put cut-up chicken and onion into the water and cook slowly until tender, add salt. Remove chicken, cut the meat into small (1-inch) pieces and return to broth, together with corn, which has been cut from the cob, celery and seasoning. Continue to simmer. Make rivels by combining 1 cup flour, a pinch of salt, 1 egg and a little milk. Mix well with fork or fingers to form small crumbs. Drop these into the soup, also the chopped, hard-boiled eggs. Boil for 15 minutes longer.

CORN SOUP *WITH* RIVELS

- **3 cups fresh or canned corn**
- **2 qts. water**

- **1 cup rich milk**
- **1⅓ cups flour**
- **1 egg**
- **3 tblsp. butter**
- **1½ tsp. salt**
- **parsley**

Cook corn in water for 10 minutes. Make a batter by mixing egg, flour and milk together. Pour this batter through a colander, letting it drop into the boiling corn. Add butter and salt. Cook slowly in a covered pan for 3 minutes. Garnish with chopped parsley. Soup should be eaten immediately after rivels are cooked.

CHICKEN NOODLE SOUP

- **4 lb. chicken**
- **2½ qts. water**
- **2½ tsp. salt**
- **3 cups cooked noodles**

Cut a young stewing chicken into serving pieces, bring to a boil and simmer for 2½ hours, adding water as needed. Skim off the fat and add:

- **1 tsp. peppercorns**
- **1 small onion, sliced**
- **1 carrot, sliced**
- **1 bay leaf**
- **1 tblsp. parsley, chopped**
- **salt and pepper**

Bring to boil again and add noodles, preferably home made noodles. Cook for 20 minutes longer.

PENNSYLVANIA DUTCH

Main Dishes

CREAMED CABBAGE *and* DRIED BEEF

- **½ large head cabbage**
- **¼ lb. dried beef**
- **1½ cups white sauce**
- **½ cup buttered crumbs**

Chop cabbage coarsely and cook in salted water until tender, then drain. Chop the dried beef and soak in a little warm water for 10 minutes. Grease a casserole and in it place alternate layers of cabbage and dried beef. Pour the white sauce over it and top with buttered bread crumbs. Bake in moderate oven (350-f) 25 minutes.

DUTCH NOODLE CHEESE RING

- **1 cup egg noodles**
- **3 tblsp. butter**
- **3 tblsp. flour**

- **½ tsp. salt**
- **½ tsp. paprika**
- **1½ cups milk**
- **2 eggs, well beaten**
- **Swiss cheese (¼ to ½ lb.)**

Boil noodles in salted water until tender. Drain and place in well-greased ring mold. Melt the butter, add flour and blend smooth. Stir in milk and cook, stirring constantly until it thickens. Add seasoning and cheese cut in small pieces. Cook until cheese melts. To ½ of the sauce add the well-beaten eggs and mix well. Pour this over the noodles. Set mold in pan of hot water and bake in moderate (350-f) oven 45 minutes. Unmold on large platter, pour over the remaining hot cheese sauce. Fill center with peas, and carrots or spinach.

POTATO FILLING

- **2 cups mashed potatoes**
- **1 egg, beaten**
- **1 qt. stale bread, cubed**
- **2 tblsp. butter**
- **1 onion, minced**
- **½ cup celery, diced**
- **1 tblsp. minced parsley**
- **1 tsp. salt**
- **pinch of pepper**

Put the beaten egg into the mashed potatoes and mix well. Melt the butter in a large skillet and saute the onion and celery. Stir in the bread crumbs to toast for a few minutes, stirring constantly. Add all the other ingredients, combine with the potatoes and mix thoroughly.

DUTCH CABBAGE ROLLS

- **1 lb. ground beef**
- **⅓ cup rice, uncooked**
- **1 egg**
- **1 onion, chopped fine**
- **2 tblsp. shortening**
- **Juice of 1 lemon**
- **1 can tomato soup**

- **½ cup celery, chopped**
- **1 tsp. sugar**
- **1 tsp. parsley, minced**
- **6 cabbage leaves**
- **salt and pepper**

Combine meat, salt, pepper, rice and egg, mix well. For the sauce: saute onion in the butter until soft. Add tomato soup and equal amount of water to onion, also celery, parsley, lemon juice, sugar, salt and pepper. Cook for 10 minutes. Wash the cabbage leaves and boil until tender. Put equal amounts of the meat mixture into cabbage leaves, roll tightly and secure with toothpicks. Place rolls in sauce pan, pour sauce over them, cover pan and cook very slowly for 3 hours.

DUCK UN KRAUT

Prepare a young duck for roasting. Place in a roasting pan and add 2 quarts of sauerkraut, 1 cup of water and 3 tablespoons granulated sugar. Cover and bake until duck is tender and golden brown. Serve with creamy mashed potatoes.

PORK POT PIE *WITH* DUMPLINGS

- **8 loin pork chops**
- **2 qts. water**
- **1 dumpling recipe**
- **4 medium potatoes**
- **1 lb. sausage in casing**

Boil the pork chops in water for ½ hour. Then add the potatoes cut in half and the sausage cut in 1 inch pieces. Cook until potatoes are almost done. Drop well-beaten dumpling dough into the boiling meat mixture, cover and cook 10 minutes.

SAUERBRATEN

2 inch thick piece of chuck, pot roast or tender boiling beef. Place in dish or bowl and cover with solution of half vinegar and half water, put in two large onions sliced. Do this two or three days before the meat is wanted. On the day before it is to be cooked cut 3 or 4 slices of bacon into 1" pieces and chop fine 1 tablespoon of the onion which has been soaking in the vinegar. Cut holes in the meat 1 or 2 inches apart and

stuff bits of the bacon and chopped onion into the holes. Put the meat back into the solution, add 1 tablespoon whole cloves and 1 teaspoon whole allspice. Bake the meat as a pot roast in part of the solution, until tender. Use more of the solution, adding sugar to taste, in making the gravy which will be almost black.

HORSERADISH SAUCE

For Boiled beef or Corned beef

- **2 tblsp. butter**
- **2 tblsp. flour**
- **1 cup milk**
- **¼ cup grated horseradish**
- **¼ tsp. dry mustard**
- **salt and pepper**

Melt butter, remove from heat and stir in flour. Add the milk gradually, stirring constantly, until mixture boils and thickens. Add salt and pepper and cook for 3 minutes more. Add the grated horseradish and dry mustard and blend well. Keep hot in double boiler. Serve on slices of boiled beef or corned beef.

SCHNITZEL MEAT

- **1½ lbs. veal steak cut in cubes**
- **2 tblsp. shortening**
- **2 tblsp. flour**
- **1 cup tomato juice**
- **2 carrots, diced**
- **1 small onion, chopped fine.**
- **Salt and pepper**
- **Flour**

Dredge meat with flour and season. Melt shortening (preferably bacon fat) and brown the meat in it. Remove meat from the pan, stir in the flour and blend. Add the tomato juice and stir well until mixture thickens. Add meat, carrots and onion. Cover closely and simmer for 45 minutes.

CHICKEN POT PIE

- **1 cup flour**
- **1 egg**

- **2 tsp. baking powder**
- **½ egg shell of water**
- **small teaspoon salt**

Mix the above ingredients, roll out and cut in two inch squares. Flour chicken and fry in butter. Put layers of chicken, potato slices, sliced onion and squares of pot-pie dough. Barely cover with boiling water and cook for two hours.

HAM *AND* NOODLES IN CASSEROLE

- **½ lb. noodles**
- **1½ cups cooked ham, diced**
- **2 eggs, beaten**
- **1½ cups milk**

Cook noodles in salted boiling water until soft. Pour into colander, drain and wash. Into a well greased casserole put alternate layers of noodles and ham. Beat eggs with the milk and pour over noodles and ham. Set casserole in pan of hot water and bake in moderate oven (350-f) for 30 minutes.

CHICKEN FRICASSEE

- **chicken cut up**
- **butter for frying**
- **2 tablespoons flour**
- **2 tablespoons butter**
- **boiled rice**
- **2 cups water**
- **12 small white onions**
- **small pinch each of thyme,**
- **celery salt and sage**

Roll chicken pieces in flour and brown in butter. Add remaining ingredients and cook until tender, adding water so that there are 2 cups at end of cooking. Make gravy by adding 3 tablespoons of hot liquid to yolk of an egg. Stir thoroughly, then return to rest of liquid and cook five minutes. Pour over steamed rice.

BEEF POT PIE

- **2 lbs. stewing beef**

- **6 medium potatoes**
- **pot pie dough**
- **2 onions**
- **chopped parsley**
- **salt and pepper**

Cut the beef into 1" cubes cover with water, season and boil until tender. Peel potatoes, cut in ¼" slices and slice the onion. Into the hot broth drop layers of potatoes, onions, a sprinkling of parsley and dough squares alternately, ending with dough on top. Cover and boil for 20 minutes. Stir meat thru pot pie.

For the pot pie dough:

To 2 cups of flour add a little salt, 1 egg, beaten and enough milk to make a stiff dough. Roll out thin (⅛") on floured board and cut into 2" squares. Equally good with veal or pork.

PENNSYLVANIA DUTCH BEEF WITH ONIONS

- **1½ lbs. boiled beef**
- **2 tablespoons butter**
- **1 tablespoon vinegar**
- **1 onion**
- **2 tablespoons flour**
- **1 pinch of pepper**
- **½ cup meat stock**
- **salt**

Mince the onion. Simmer in butter until soft. Add flour and simmer until brown. To this add vinegar, salt, pepper and meat stock and let come to a boil. Cut the meat in slices and serve hot, with the onion sauce.

WIENER SCHNITZEL (Veal Cutlet)

- **2 lbs. veal steak**
- **1 egg, beaten**
- **salt**
- **bread crumbs**
- **lemon juice**
- **pepper**

Veal should be about ½ inch thick and cut into serving portions. Season with salt and pepper. Dip pieces in bread crumbs, then into the beaten egg and again in the crumbs. Let stand in the refrigerator a while before cooking. Brown in hot fat on both sides, cover and simmer for 30 minutes. Sprinkle with lemon juice.

HAMBURGER DINNER

- **1 lb. hamburger**
- **3 cups potatoes, sliced**
- **salt**
- **1 small head cabbage**
- **1 cup milk**
- **pepper**

Shred cabbage and put ½ of it in a greased casserole. Add ½ of the sliced potatoes and half of the hamburger a sprinkle of salt and pepper. Add remaining half in the same manner. Pour on the milk and bake in a moderate oven (350-f) for 2 hours.

CHICKEN BAKED *IN* CREAM

- **1 young chicken, cut up**
- **½ cup flour**
- **1½ tsp. salt**
- **⅛ tsp. pepper**
- **3 tblsp. butter**
- **1½ cups cream, sweet or sour**

Sprinkle the pieces of chicken with salt and pepper and dredge in flour. Melt butter and fry chicken until a golden brown on all sides. Place the chicken in a casserole, pour the cream over it. Cover and bake in a moderate oven (350-f) for 2 hours. Serve with gravy made from the pan fryings left after frying the chicken.

DUTCH MEAT LOAF

- **2½ lbs. hamburg**
- **2½ cups bread crumbs**
- **1 cup cheese (cubed small)**
- **salt and pepper**
- **½ green pepper, chopped**
- **1 small onion, chopped**
- **2 eggs**
- **1 cup catsup**

Mix all ingredients, form into two loaves. Pour some catsup over top of loaves. Bake at 350 until done.

LIVER NOODLES (Leberknoedel)

- **1 lb. calf's liver**
- **1 onion**
- **1 tablespoon butter**
- **salt and pepper**
- **2 eggs**
- **½ cup flour**
- **¼ teaspoon cloves**
- **¼ teaspoon marjoram**

Simmer the liver in boiling water for 30 minutes. Then trim off any skin or ligaments and grind the liver fine. Season. Mince the onion, add the butter, beat the eggs and add them. Work into this paste the flour, using enough to make the paste quite stiff. Form into small balls and poach them in any meat soup for 15 minutes. Serve them swimming in the soup.

STUFFED PEPPERS

- **1½ lbs. ground beef and pork**
- **6 green peppers**
- **1 can tomato soup**
- **3 tblsp. rice, uncooked**
- **2 eggs, beaten**
- **½ tsp. salt**

Mix the meat, rice, eggs and seasoning together. Cut tops off the peppers and soak in hot water for a couple of minutes. Scoop out seeds and fill with the meat mixture. Stand them in baking pan, pour the tomato soup over them and bake in slow oven (300-f) for 1 hour.

MEAT PIE

- **1½ cups leftover meat**
- **3 tblsp. flour**
- **¼ cup drippings**
- **1 cup milk**
- **1 tblsp. grated onion**
- **⅓ cup chopped pepper**
- **salt**
- **pepper**

Add flour to drippings and blend, add milk gradually and cook, stirring constantly until it thickens. Stir in the salt, onion and green pepper. Mix cut-up meat into the gravy and pour it into pastry lined baking dish. Top with crust and bake in hot oven (425-f) for 25 minutes.

STUFFED ACORN SQUASH

- **3 acorn squash**
- **⅓ cup molasses**
- **1 tsp. salt**
- **1 lb. pork sausage**
- **1 tsp. sage**
- **bread crumbs**

Wash squash and cut in halves, remove seeds. Put a tablespoon of molasses in each half, sprinkle with salt and a pinch of powdered sage (if the sausage does not contain sage). Fill the cavity with sausage and top with bread crumbs. Place the squash halves in a baking pan, add about an inch of water to the pan. Cover and bake in hot oven (400-f) for 40 minutes. Remove cover and brown.

BAKED SPARERIBS *AND* SAUERKRAUT

with Dumplings

- **Spareribs**
- **sauerkraut**
- **2 cups flour**
- **1 egg, beaten**
- **1 tsp. baking powder**
- **1 cup milk**

Cut spareribs into serving portions and place in the bottom of roasting pan. Add the sauerkraut and a little liquid. Cover and bake in moderate oven (350-f) 1½ hours. Make dumplings by combining flour, baking powder, milk and egg. Drop by spoonfuls on sauerkraut, cover tightly and bake for 20 minutes.

SOUSE

Use 3 pigs feet or about 2 lbs. Scrape, wash and clean thoroughly. Place in stew pan with 1 chopped onion, ½ cup chopped celery and cover with cold water. Let it come to a boil, then reduce heat and simmer until meat is tender and comes easily from the bone. Pick meat from the bones, strain liquid, which should measure a scant 3 cups. (If less add water). Put meat and liquid into a bowl. Add 3 tblsp. strong cider vinegar, ¾ tsp. salt, black pepper and several thin slices of lemon. Chill overnight, remove surplus fat from the top. Turn out on a platter and serve with lemon slices and parsley.

PORK AND KRAUT (Speck Un Kraut)

- **2 or 3 lbs. fresh pork**
- **1 qt. sauerkraut**
- **water**
- **salt and pepper**

Put pork in large stew pan and cover with cold water, cook slowly for 1 hour. Add the sauerkraut making sure there is enough liquid in the pan to cover. Cook slowly for another hour. Season to taste. Serve with mashed or boiled potatoes.

MOCK DUCK

- **1 thick round steak**
- **2 cups bread crumbs**
- **1 tblsp. onion minced**
- **2 eggs**
- **½ cup milk**
- **1 tblsp. butter**
- **1 tsp. salt**
- **poultry seasoning**

To make dressing beat eggs, add milk and pour over bread crumbs. Add the onion, seasoning and work in the butter mixing thoroughly. Spread the dressing over the meat and roll up carefully. Fasten with skewers or tie with string. Place in a greased pan and bake in medium hot oven (375-f) for 1½ hours. Slice to serve.

HOG MAW

- **1 pig's stomach**
- **2 lbs. smoked sausage meat, diced.**
- **3 cups boiled potatoes, diced**
- **3 cups sliced apples**
- **2½ cups bread crumbs**

- **1 medium onion, chopped**
- **2 cups chopped celery**
- **chopped parsley**
- **salt and pepper**

Clean stomach well and soak in salt water. Combine all ingredients and mix well. Stuff the stomach with the mixture and sew up the opening. Simmer for 2 hours in a large kettle with water to cover. Remove to baking pan with hot fat, brown in hot oven (400-f) basting frequently. Slice with sharp knife.

SCHNITZ UN KNEPP

Boil a 3 lb. piece of ham for two hours. Pick over and clean 1 qt. of dried apples; soak in enough water to cover. When meat has boiled for the stated time, add dried apples and water in which they have been soaking and continue to boil for another hour. Prepare dumpling batter as follows:

- **2 cups flour**
- **1 egg**
- **4 teaspoons baking powder**
- **3 tblsp. melted shortening**
- **¼ teaspoon pepper**
- **1 tablespoon milk**
- **1 teaspoon salt**

Sift together the dry ingredients and mix the dough with egg, which has been well beaten, the melted shortening and the milk. Drop batter by spoonfuls into the boiling liquor of the ham and apples. Cover tightly and cook for 15 minutes. Raisins may be added if desired.

HAM *AND* GREEN BEANS

- **2 or 3 lbs. ham or ham bone**
- **1 qt. green string beans**
- **potatoes**
- **salt and pepper**

Place ham in large pot and cover with water. Cook slowly for a couple of hours (less if the ham is tenderized) keeping plenty of water on the ham. Clean and break-up the string beans, put them in with ham and cook for 25 minutes more. Add the potatoes, which have been pared and cut-up, and cook slowly until ready. Season to taste.

SAUSAGE PATTIES

Equal amount of lean and fat fresh pork, ground. To each pound of this mixture, add 1 teaspoon salt, ⅛ teaspoon pepper, pinch each of sage and thyme. Add one egg beaten, mould into cakes and fry until brown. Wonderful with pancakes or waffles.

DUTCH MEAT ROLLS (Boova Shenkel)

- **2½ lbs. beef**
- **10 potatoes**
- **2 tablespoons butter**
- **2 tablespoons minced parsley**
- **1 chopped onion**
- **½ teaspoon salt**
- **½ cup milk**
- **3 eggs**
- **2½ cups flour**
- **2 teaspoons baking powder**
- **1 tablespoon shortening**
- **1 tablespoon butter**

After seasoning the meat with salt and pepper, stew the meat for two hours. Then make dough with flour, baking powder, salt and the shortening. Mix into a pie-crust dough. Roll into a dozen circles 8 to 10 inches in diameter. Steam the potatoes, pared and sliced thin; add salt and pepper, 2 tablespoons of butter; the parsley and onions and then beat lightly the three eggs into the mixture. Put this mixture on the circles of dough after it has stood a little while. Fold half the circle of dough over like a half moon and press edges together tightly. Drop these into the pot with the meat and stew water. Cover tightly and cook for 30 minutes. Into a frying pan put a couple of tablespoons of fat skimmed from the stew before putting in the dough rolls, add to this 1 tablespoon of butter. In this brown small cubes of hard bread and stir in a half cup of milk. Pour this milk sauce over the Meat rolls when serving.

SCRAPPLE

- **½ lb. chopped raw meat (beef or pork)**
- **1¼ teaspoons salt**
- **⅛ teaspoon pepper**
- **1 cup corn meal**
- **1 medium onion chopped**
- **1¼ qts. water**

Brown onion slowly in a little fat. Add meat, seasoning and water. Cook at simmering point 20 minutes. Add to corn meal and boil for 1 hour. Turn into a mold, cool, cut in slices and fry in fat until brown. Serve with gravy or tomato sauce.

PENNSYLVANIA DUTCH CHICKEN AND OYSTER PIE

- **1 stewing chicken**
- **1 pt. oysters**
- **¼ lb. butter**
- **salt and pepper**
- **a little flour**
- **pastry crust**

Stew chicken until tender, season with ¼ lb. butter, salt and pepper. Line deep dish with pastry crust. Pour in the stewed chicken and cover loosely with a crust in the center of which a hole the size of a tea cup has been cut. Prepare separately 1 pt. oysters, heating the liquor with a little flour and water. Season with salt, pepper and 2 tablespoons of butter. When it comes to a boil, pour over oysters. 20 minutes before pie is done, lift the top crust and put the oyster mixture in.

PENNSYLVANIA DUTCH

Vegetable Dishes

LANCASTER COUNTY BAKED CORN

To 1 cup of dried corn (ground in food chopper) pour on 2 cups of hot milk and let stand about an hour. Then add 2 beaten eggs, 1 cup milk, 1 tablespoon butter, 2 tablespoons sugar and salt to taste. Bake ½ hour in oven of 350 to 360 degrees.

SEVEN-MINUTE CABBAGE

- **2 cups milk**
- **2 teaspoons flour**
- **salt and pepper**
- **1 tablespoon butter**
- **2 cups chopped cabbage**

Heat the milk to boiling. Add butter and the cabbage. Cook seven minutes. Thicken with the flour, mixed with a little cold water.

SCALLOPED SWEET POTATOES *AND* APPLES

- **6 medium-sized sweet potatoes**
- **½ cup brown sugar**
- **1½ cups sliced apples**
- **4 tblsp. butter**
- **½ tsp. salt**
- **1 tsp. mace**

Boil sweet potatoes until tender. Slice in ¼ inch pieces. Butter baking dish and put a layer of sweet potatoes in bottom, then a layer of apples. Sprinkle with sugar, salt and mace, and dot with butter. Repeat until dish is filled, having the top layer of apples. Bake in moderate oven (350-f) for 50 minutes.

SWEET POTATO CROQUETTES

- **1 pt. mashed sweet potatoes**
- **1 tblsp. butter**
- **1 tsp. salt**
- **1 tblsp. sugar**
- **1 egg white**
- **bread crumbs**

Mash sweet potatoes very fine and add salt, sugar and melted butter. Shape into croquette rolls or patties and chill in the refrigerator for a half hour. Then roll in bread crumbs, dip in the egg white, slightly beaten, and in the crumbs again. Bake in a shallow, greased baking dish for 20 minutes, in hot oven (400-f). For a modern variation of this old recipe, place a marshmallow in the center of each with the potato mixture coating it completely.

SCHNITZEL BEANS

- **4 slices bacon**
- **1 qt. string beans**
- **3 medium onions, sliced**
- **2 cups tomatoes, chopped**
- **1 tsp. salt**

- **¼ tsp. pepper**
- **1 cup hot water**

Dice the bacon and fry until crisp. Slice the onions and fry until soft. Cut the beans into small (1-inch) pieces and brown them slightly with the bacon and onions. Add the tomatoes, seasoning and boiling water. Cover and cook very slowly until beans are tender. Add water if necessary, so there will be a little sauce to serve with the beans.

FRIED TOMATOES

- **4 tomatoes**
- **3 tblsp. hot fat and butter**
- **2 tblsp. brown sugar**
- **Flour**
- **½ cup milk**
- **salt and pepper**

Cut large, solid, ripe tomatoes in ½ inch slices. Dredge thickly with flour. Fry quickly in 2 tablespoons of hot drippings or butter, browning well on both sides. Remove to serving platter, sprinkle with salt, pepper and brown sugar. Keep warm. Add 1 tablespoon of butter to the pan fryings and blend in a tablespoon of flour. Add the milk and cook, stirring constantly. It should be about the consistency of thick cream. Pour it over the tomatoes and serve.

PARSNIP PATTIES

- **6 or 7 parsnips**
- **1 tablespoon butter or shortening**
- **2 eggs**
- **½ cup bread crumbs, dry**
- **1 teaspoon sugar**
- **½ teaspoon salt**
- **little pepper**
- **milk**

Boil parsnips in salted water. When soft, peel and remove the core then mash. Add shortening, bread crumbs, salt, pepper, sugar and 1 egg and the white of the other, beaten. Mix well and form into cakes. Beat the remaining egg yolk with a little milk added. Dip the cakes into the egg, roll in corn meal or bread crumbs and fry to a nice brown.

SCALLOPED POTATOES

- **6 potatoes, sliced**
- **1 onion, chopped**
- **2 tsp. salt**
- **pepper**
- **3 tblsp. butter**
- **2 tblsp. flour**
- **2 cups hot milk**
- **¾ cup grated cheese**

Melt butter in double boiler or sauce pan. Add flour, seasoning and stir smooth. Slowly add the hot milk stirring constantly. When it thickens melt the grated cheese in the sauce. Into a buttered baking dish or casserole put layers of the sliced potatoes, onions and cheese sauce, repeating until all ingredients are used. Bake in a moderate oven (350-f) for 1 hour.

FRIED EGG PLANT

Pare egg plant and cut in slices ½ inch thick. Soak slices in salt water for about an hour. Drain and wipe dry. Dip slices in beaten egg and roll in fine bread or cracker crumbs. Fry in hot fat (or deep fat) until well browned on both sides. Serve with catsup or tomato sauce.

SWEET *AND* SOUR BEETS

- **3 cups beets, diced**
- **1 cup beet water**
- **1 tblsp. sugar**
- **¼ cup vinegar**
- **2 tsp. butter**
- **1 tblsp. corn starch**

Cut off beet tops leaving 2 inches of the stems. Clean well, place in pot and cover with boiling water. Cook until tender, slip off the outer skins and dice. Strain and save 1 cup of the water in which beets were cooked. Add sugar, vinegar and butter. Thicken with 1 tablespoon of corn starch and cook to the consistency of cream. Add the diced beets, salt and pepper and heat.

SCALLOPED TOMATOES

- **3 cups tomatoes canned or fresh**
- **1 medium cucumber pared and sliced**
- **salt**
- **1 small onion, sliced**
- **½ cup bread crumbs, buttered**
- **½ cup grated cheese**
- **pepper**

Into a greased baking dish or casserole place a layer of tomatoes, add half the cucumber and onion slices and half of the crumbs. Repeat with more tomatoes and remaining cucumbers, onions and crumbs. Top with tomatoes and sprinkle with cheese. Bake in moderate oven, (375-f) 40 minutes.

DUTCH POTATO CROQUETTES

- **1½ cups cold mashed potatoes**
- **1 tablespoon butter**
- **1 teaspoon minced parsley**
- **2 tablespoons cream**
- **corn meal**
- **¼ teaspoon salt**
- **½ teaspoon minced onion**
- **dash of pepper**
- **1 egg**

Mix up a paste with the potatoes and butter, add the parsley, salt and pepper, cream, onion and egg. Mold into croquettes, dip into the egg white, roll in corn meal. Fry in deep fat.

RED CABBAGE (Rote Kraut)

Place 4 tablespoons bacon grease in pressure cooker, then chop fine 1 small onion in grease and brown onion to golden brown. Shred (1) 2½ lb. head of red cabbage. Mix ¼ cup vinegar with ¼ cup water and 2 tablespoons sugar.

Then place cabbage in onion and grease. Pour mixture of vinegar and sugar on cabbage. Season with salt and pepper to taste and mix lightly. Quarter 1 large pared apple and place on top of cabbage. Cook 4 min. When using an ordinary pot the cooking time is 20 minutes. This makes 10 servings.

SCALLOPED SPINACH

- **2 lbs. spinach**
- **2 cups milk**
- **4 tblsp. butter**
- **salt**
- **2 eggs, beaten**
- **2 cups bread crumbs**
- **½ cup chopped bacon**
- **pepper**

Wash spinach thoroughly. Drain and cook with a little water in covered pot, over moderate heat for 8 to 10 minutes. Drain and chop the spinach. Add milk, the beaten eggs, 1½ cups of the bread crumbs, melted butter, salt and pepper then mix well. Sprinkle the remaining ½ cup bread crumbs and the chopped bacon, on the top. Bake in moderate oven (350-f) 35 minutes.

FRESH PEAS *AND* NEW POTATOES

- **3 cups fresh peas**
- **12 small new potatoes**
- **1½ tsp. salt**
- **1½ cups milk**
- **1½ tsp. flour**
- **2 tblsp. butter**

Cook potatoes and peas in separate pans, in salted water until soft and almost free of water. Mix the peas and potatoes and add the milk. Bring to the boiling point then add the butter and flour which have been blended smooth and cook until thickened.

CORN PUDDING

- **1 can golden crushed corn**
- **2 eggs, slightly beaten**
- **2 tbs. flour**
- **2 tbs. sugar**
- **1 cup milk**
- **salt and pepper**
- **lots of butter**

Mix all ingredients together. Place in buttered casserole. Bake in slow oven 300 degrees for one hour.

SWEET *AND* SOUR CELERY

- **2 cups celery, diced**
- **1 tsp. salt**
- **2 tblsp. sugar**
- **2 tblsp. vinegar**
- **2 tblsp. flour**
- **1 egg**
- **1 cup water**
- **¼ cup sour cream**

Cut up celery and cook in a little salt water until soft and almost dry. Make a dressing of the egg, flour, sugar, vinegar and water, bring to a boil and when it thickens add the sour cream. Pour this over the celery, heat and serve.

HOME BAKED BEANS

- **2 cups navy beans**
- **1½ tsp. salt**
- **1 small onion, minced**
- **4 tblsp. molasses**
- **1 tsp. dry mustard**
- **4 tblsp. catsup**
- **¼ lb. salt pork**
- **or 4 slices bacon**

Soak beans over night in cold water. Drain, add 1½ qts. of fresh water, the Onion and cook slowly until skins burst. Drain save the liquid. Mix molasses, seasoning and catsup with 1 cup of the liquid. Put half the salt pork or bacon in bottom of bean pot or baking dish, add the beans and top with remainder of pork or bacon. Pour molasses mixture over beans, add more liquid to cover. Bake covered for 5 hours in slow oven (300-f). Uncover for the last 30 minutes. Add water if necessary, while cooking.

CABBAGE, SWEET *AND* SOUR

- **cabbage**
- **1 egg**

- **¼ cup vinegar**
- **1 tablespoon sugar**
- **1 teaspoon salt**

Shred cabbage rather finely. Put in sauce pan and sprinkle with salt. Cover pan and place over low heat and steam until tender. Beat the egg, add the vinegar, sugar and salt and pour over the steamed cabbage. Heat five minutes and serve at once.

CORN FRITTERS

1 cup ground dried corn, add 1¼ cups milk (or part water); let stand ½ hour or longer, add ½ teaspoon salt, ½ teaspoon sugar, 1 teaspoon baking powder, ½ cup flour, 1 egg, well beaten, and fry to a golden brown.

HASHED BROWN POTATOES

- **6 medium, cold boiled potatoes**
- **shortening**
- **3 raw green peppers**
- **¼ teaspoon celery salt**
- **salt and pepper**

Chop potatoes fine, season with celery salt, salt and pepper to taste. Remove seeds and stem from pepper, wash drain and chop fine. Mix with potatoes. Put about 1 tablespoon of melted shortening in pan and when hot, add potatoes and cook slowly. When partly brown, fold into omelet shape in one side of pan. Fry until a rich brown.

BAKED LIMA BEANS

- **2 cups dried limas**
- **4 slices bacon or salt pork**
- **1 medium onion**
- **1 green pepper**
- **1 cup canned tomatoes**
- **2 tsp. salt**
- **1 tsp. mustard**
- **2 tblsp. brown sugar**

Soak beans overnight in cold water. Drain, add 2 quarts of fresh water and boil until tender. Pour beans in buttered casserole. Add minced pepper, onion, tomatoes and seasoning and mix. Put bacon or salt pork on top and bake, covered. Add water if necessary. Bake 2 hours at (325-f). Uncover for the last 20 minutes.

PENNSYLVANIA DUTCH

Pancakes and Fritters

APPLE RING FRITTERS

- **1 cup sifted flour**
- **1½ teaspoons baking powder**
- **2 tablespoons sugar**
- **½ teaspoon salt**
- **¾ cup milk**
- **1 egg**
- **4 large apples**

Sift dry ingredients. Add milk and egg. Beat well. Peel and core apples and slice in rings about ¼ inch thick. Dip rings in batter and drop into skillet containing ½ inch of hot melted shortening. Fry until golden brown on both sides. Drain on paper towel. Mix sugar and cinnamon together and sprinkle over fritters. Makes 16 to 20.

SOUR CHERRY FRITTERS

- **1 cup flour, sifted**
- **1 tsp. baking powder**
- **½ tsp. salt**
- **2 tblsp. sugar**
- **2 eggs, separated**
- **3 tblsp. water**
- **1 cup pitted sour cherries**

Sift together the flour, baking powder, salt and sugar. Combine the beaten egg yolks with water and mix until smooth. Fold in the stiffly-beaten egg whites and add the cherries. Drop by spoonfuls into hot fat (360-f) and cook 2 to 5 minutes or until browned. Drain on absorbent paper and serve with powdered sugar or fruit sauce. Other fruits or berries may be used.

CORN MEAL GRIDDLE CAKES

- **2 cups corn meal**
- **½ cup flour**
- **1 tsp. baking powder**
- **1 tsp. soda**
- **2 eggs**
- **2 cups buttermilk**
- **2 tblsp. butter**
- **1½ tsp. salt**

Sift flour, corn meal, baking powder, soda and salt. Sift again. Beat eggs well, add the buttermilk and combine with the dry ingredients. Beat until smooth and add melted butter. Bake on hot griddle. The "dutch" housewife rubbed the griddle with the flat part of a raw turnip cut in half, to prevent sticking. Some used a little cloth bag filled with salt. Serve with brown sugar or syrup.

CORN FRITTERS

- **2 eggs, separated**
- **2 tblsp. flour**
- **1 tblsp. sugar**
- **2 cups grated fresh corn**

Beat the egg yolks and add the flour, 1 teaspoon salt and a little pepper. Add the corn and fold in the stiffly beaten egg whites. Drop small spoonfuls on greased griddle or frying pan. Do not cook too fast.

OLD-FASHIONED FLANNEL CAKES

- **2 cups flour**
- **1 tblsp. baking powder**
- **1 tsp. salt**
- **2 cups milk**
- **2 eggs, separated**
- **2 tblsp. melted butter**

Sift together in a bowl the flour, salt and baking powder. Beat the egg yolks and add the milk. Pour milk mixture slowly into the dry ingredients and beat to a smooth batter. Add the melted butter then fold in the stiffly beaten egg whites. Bake on hot griddle. Makes about 12 cakes.

FRIED CORN MEAL MUSH

- **1 cup corn meal**
- **2 qts. boiling water**
- **1 tsp. salt**

Moisten corn meal with a little cold water and stir into the salted boiling water. Cook over slow fire, stirring often, for 45 minutes. (Most of the corn meal sold today has been processed to cook much faster, so follow the directions.) Pour the hot corn meal into a greased loaf pan or glass baking dish. Let stand, uncovered, until cold and firm. Cut into slices, dip in flour and fry in hot fat until browned. Serve with syrup. Wonderful with sausage.

PEACH FRITTERS

- **½ cup sugar**
- **2 eggs, well beaten**
- **⅓ cup butter**
- **2 cups flour**
- **3 tsp. baking powder**
- **½ tsp. salt**
- **1 cup milk**
- **½ tsp. lemon juice**
- **½ tsp. vanilla**
- **1½ cups chopped peaches, fresh or canned**
- **whipped cream**

Cream the butter and sugar, add the eggs and beat thoroughly. Sift dry ingredients together and add the milk slowly. Fold in peaches, lemon juice and vanilla. Drop by teaspoonfuls into hot fat. Fry golden brown. Serve with whipped cream or sprinkle with powdered sugar.

GERMAN EGG PANCAKES

- **5 eggs, separated**
- **½ cup milk**
- **1 cup flour, sifted**

Put the yolks of 5 eggs in a bowl and beat until very light. Add the milk and flour gradually and mix into a smooth batter which is not too thick. Fold in the stiffly beaten egg whites. Drop large spoonfuls on a hot greased griddle. Serve hot sprinkled with sugar or spread with currant or other tart jelly or jam.

POTATO PANCAKES

- **2 eggs, separated**
- **1 cup mashed potatoes**
- **½ cup flour**
- **1 cup milk**
- **2 tsp. baking powder**

Add egg yolks to the mashed potatoes and mix well. Add the flour and baking powder alternately with the milk until smooth. Fold in the stiffly beaten egg whites and drop spoonfuls on hot greased griddle or skillet. Finely chopped onion is sometimes sprinkled on the batter on griddle before turning. Serve hot with meat.

PENNSYLVANIA DUTCH

Fastnacht Day

Doughnuts

POTATO DOUGHNUTS

- **¾ cup sugar**
- **2 eggs**
- **1 cup mashed potatoes**
- **½ cup sweet milk**
- **2½ cups flour**
- **1½ tblsp. shortening**
- **½ tsp. salt**
- **⅛ tsp. nutmeg**
- **1 tblsp. baking powder**

Beat mashed potatoes, add melted shortening, beaten eggs and milk. Sift dry ingredients together and add to the liquid. Dough should be soft yet firm enough to roll. Separate dough into 2 parts and roll each out to thickness of ¾ inch. Cut with doughnut cutter and cook in deep fat (365-f) fry to golden brown. Drain on absorbent paper. Dust with powdered sugar or sugar and cinnamon mixture.

BLUEBERRY MUFFINS

- **⅓ cup butter**
- **¾ cup sugar**
- **1 egg beaten lightly**
- **1 cup milk**
- **2 level cups flour**
- **4 level teaspoons baking powder**
- **½ teaspoon salt**
- **1 cup blueberries**

Cream butter and sugar. Add fruit and egg, then milk and flour sifted with baking powder and salt. Bake in muffin tins.

JOHNNY CAKE

- **1½ cups yellow corn meal**
- **¾ cup flour, sifted**
- **1½ tsp. baking powder**
- **¾ tsp. baking soda**

- **1 tsp. salt**
- **2 tblsp. sugar**
- **2 eggs, beaten**
- **1¼ cups sour milk or buttermilk**
- **¼ cup shortening, melted**

Sift flour, corn meal, baking powder, soda, salt and sugar together. Combine eggs and sour milk (or buttermilk) and add to the flour mixture. Mix well and stir in the shortening. Bake in greased 8 × 8 × 2-inch pan, in moderately hot oven (375-f) 40 minutes.

BRAN MUFFINS

- **1 cup flour**
- **3½ tsp. baking powder**
- **½ tsp. salt**
- **2 tblsp. brown sugar**
- **1 cup bran**
- **1 egg, beaten**
- **⅔ cup milk**
- **2 tblsp. shortening, melted**

Sift the flour, baking powder and salt. Stir in the sugar and bran. Combine the beaten egg, milk and melted shortening. Add to the dry ingredients and mix quickly. Turn into greased muffin pans and bake in hot oven (425-f) 25 minutes. Raisins or chopped dried prunes may be added.

BACON MUFFINS

- **2 cups flour**
- **1 tablespoon sugar**
- **3 tablespoons melted shortening**
- **1 cup milk**
- **3 teaspoons baking powder**
- **½ teaspoon salt**
- **1 egg**
- **½ cup bits crisp bacon**

Sift flour, add sugar, salt and baking powder and sift again, add beaten egg and milk. Add melted shortening beating in quickly. Add bits of crisped bacon. Bake in hot (425 degree) oven for 15 to 20 minutes. Serve with orange marmalade.

FASTNACHTS—Raised Doughnuts

For the Sponge:

- **1 cake yeast**
- **2 cups lukewarm water**
- **4 scant cups sifted flour**

At night break and soak yeast in lukewarm water for 20 minutes. Mix with flour to a thick batter. Cover, let rise in warm place overnight until doubled.

For the Dough:

- **½ cup shortening**
- **⅜ cup sugar**
- **1½ teaspoons salt**
- **2 eggs**
- **½ teaspoon ground nutmeg**
- **5 cups or more of flour**

In the morning cream together the shortening, sugar and salt. Add this to the risen sponge, with the beaten eggs and spice. Stir in as much flour as mixture will take up readily, making a rather soft dough. Mix well. Let rise until doubled in bulk. If desired, stir down and let rise again until nearly doubled. Turn onto floured board, pat or roll until ⅓ inch thick and cut with doughnut cutter. Cover to prevent drying and let rise until doubled. Fry in deep hot fat about 375 degrees. If no thermometer is at hand, test temperature with 1 inch square of bread, which should brown in 1 minute.

Becky... fill the pitcher, the milk is all

CRULLERS

- **2 eggs**
- **½ cup cream, sweet or sour**
- **½ cup milk**
- **1 tsp. baking soda**
- **1 tsp. salt**
- **¼ cup sugar**

- **3½ to 4 cups flour**

Beat the eggs, add cream and milk. Sift dry ingredients and combine with liquid, using just enough flour to make dough that can be rolled, but still remain soft. Mix well and let stand for 2 hours. Turn out on floured board and roll to ¼ in. thick. Cut into strips 6" × 1". Fry in deep fat (360-f) until brown on both sides. Drain on absorbent paper and dust with powdered sugar, if you wish.

TANGLE BRITCHES

An old York County Recipe

- **½ lb. butter**
- **1 cup sugar**
- **6 eggs, beaten**
- **½ tsp. cinnamon**
- **about 5 cups flour**

Cream together the butter and sugar. Add the eggs beating well. Sift in the cinnamon and enough flour to make a stiff dough. Roll out the dough very thin on a floured board to about ⅛ inch thick. Cut into rectangular pieces 3 inches by 5 inches. Make 5 cuts lengthwise in the dough ½ inch apart and 4½ inches long, so that the rectangle remains in one piece. Fry in hot deep fat (360-f) for 2 minutes or until they bob up to the top of the hot grease. When dropping them into the fryer, pick up the 1st, 3rd and 5th strips and pull them upward. Let the 2nd, 4th and 6th sag downward so that in frying they get all fahuudelt (tangled) or as the dutch say, all through each other. Dust with powdered sugar or dribble molasses over them and eat hot.

SHOO-FLY PIE

For the crumb part:

- **¼ cup shortening**
- **1½ cups flour**
- **1 cup brown sugar**

Work the above ingredients together.

For the liquid part:

- **¾ teaspoon baking soda**

- **⅛ teaspoon nutmeg**
- **a little ginger, cinnamon and cloves**
- **¼ teaspoon salt**
- **¾ cup molasses**
- **¾ cup hot water**

Mix well together and add hot water. Into an unbaked pie shell, combine the crumbs and liquid in alternate layers with crumbs on bottom and top. Bake 15 minutes at 450 degrees, then 20 minutes at 350 degrees.

GRANDMA'S CRUMB OR SUGAR PIE

- **2 cups flour**
- **1 heaping cup brown sugar**
- **1½ tblsp. shortening**
- **1 tsp. soda**
- **½ cup buttermilk or sour cream**
- **salt**
- **1 9-inch, unbaked pastry shell**

Combine sugar, flour and soda. Cut in the shortening and blend well. Add the liquid and rub into coarse crumbs. Put crumbs loosely into the unbaked pie shell. Bake in moderate oven (375-f) for 40 minutes. This is a breakfast treat especially good for dunking in coffee.

FUNNEL CAKES (Drechter Kuche)

- **3 eggs**
- **2 cups milk**
- **¼ cup sugar**
- **3 to 4 cups flour**
- **½ tsp. salt**
- **2 tsps. baking powder**

Beat eggs and add sugar and milk. Sift half the flour, salt and baking powder together and add to milk and egg mixture. Beat the batter smooth and add only as much more flour as needed. Batter should be thin enough to run thru a funnel. Drop from funnel into deep, hot fat (375-f). Spirals and endless intricate shapes can be made by swirling and criss-crossing while controlling the funnel spout with a finger. Serve hot with molasses, tart jelly, jam or sprinkle with powdered sugar.

SALLY LUNN

- **2 cups flour, sifted**
- **3 tsp. baking powder**
- **½ tsp. salt**
- **3 tblsp. sugar**
- **2 eggs, separated**
- **½ cup milk**
- **½ cup shortening, melted**

Sift flour, baking powder, salt and sugar. Combine the beaten egg yolks and milk and add to the flour mixture, stirring only until mixed. Add shortening, fold in the stiffly beaten egg whites. Turn into greased 9 inch square pan and bake in moderate oven (350-f) about 30 minutes. Cut into 3 inch squares.

QUICK COFFEE CAKE

- **2¼ cups flour, sifted**
- **1 cup milk**
- **3½ tsp. baking powder**
- **1 tsp. salt**
- **⅓ cup shortening**
- **⅓ cup sugar**
- **1 egg**

Sift together flour, baking powder and salt. Cream shortening and sugar beating until fluffy. Add egg, beat well and then the milk. Add the flour mixture, stirring just enough to moisten. Turn into greased 8 inch square baking pan. Top with:

- **¼ cup butter**
- **¼ cup sugar**
- **1 cup dry bread crumbs**
- **1 tsp. cinnamon**

Cream butter and sugar, well. Add bread crumbs and cinnamon. Blend well and sprinkle over cake dough. Bake in moderate oven (375-f) 40 to 50 minutes. Serve hot.

Sweets and Rolls

LITTLE COFFEE CAKES
(Kleina Kaffee Kuchen)

- **½ cup shortening, half butter**
- **3 cups flour, sifted**
- **2 whole eggs and**
- **2 egg yolks**
- **3 tblsp. sugar**
- **¼ cup cream**
- **¼ cup milk**
- **1 yeast cake**

Dissolve yeast cake in ¼ cup of warm milk, add 2 tablespoons of flour and stand in warm place to rise. Cream butter and sugar, add salt and the eggs, beaten in one at a time. Add the sponge containing the yeast, the lukewarm cream and the sifted flour. Grease muffin pans and sift a little flour over them. Fill pans about ⅔ full with the batter. Set in a warm place until dough rises to the top of the pans. Bake in hot oven (400-f) for 25 minutes.

BUTTER SEMMELS

- **1 cup mashed potatoes**
- **¾ cup shortening, ½ butter**
- **1 cup sugar**
- **1 tsp. salt**
- **2 eggs**

- **1 yeast cake**
- **1 cup warm water**
- **6 cups flour**

In a mixing bowl put warm mashed potatoes, shortening, sugar and salt. Beat to a cream and add 2 eggs, the yeast cake dissolved in cup of lukewarm water. Use about 2 cups of the flour to make a thin batter. Cover and let it raise over night. When well risen add 4 cups of flour to make as stiff a dough as can be stirred well with a mixing spoon. Roll out dough to ½ inch thickness on a floured board. Cut into squares about the size of a soda cracker. Bring each of the 4 corners, of each square, to the center and pinch together. Place a small piece of butter on top of each. Put on greased baking sheets about 2 inches apart and stand in warm place to rise until very light. Bake in hot oven (400-f) for 15 to 20 minutes. While still hot, brush with melted butter and dust with powdered sugar or sugar and cinnamon mixed.

SWEET ROLL DOUGH

- **2 cakes yeast**
- **2 cups lukewarm milk**
- **½ cup lukewarm water**
- **⅔ cup butter**
- **¾ cup sugar**
- **1½ teaspoons salt**
- **2 eggs**
- **½ lemon grated ring and juice**
- **¼ teaspoon nutmeg**
- **8 cups flour**

Break and soak yeast in water until soft. Scald and then cool milk. Cream together butter, sugar and salt. Add well beaten eggs, lemon and spice. Add lukewarm milk to yeast and mix with half the flour. Work in butter and sugar mixture and enough flour to knead into a smooth dough. Keep it as soft as can be handled readily. Let rise over night at about 80 degrees. As soon as dough is fully doubled in bulk, knead down and let rise again for an hour. Makes three dozen.

CRUMB CAKE

- **½ cup sugar**
- **½ teaspoon cinnamon**
- **¼ cup chopped nuts**
- **¾ cup flour**
- **3 tablespoons melted butter**

Combine the dry ingredients. Work in melted butter until crumbs are formed. Add nuts. Sprinkle over top of coffee cake dough and bake.

DUTCH STICKY BUNS

Roll ⅓ of the sweet dough into an oblong sheet, ¼ inch thick. Brush with butter and sprinkle with brown sugar and cinnamon. Roll up and cut off 1 inch slices. Place cut side down in greased pan. Brush tops with butter. Let rise until double. Sprinkle with brown sugar and cinnamon and chopped pecans or pour corn syrup in the bottom of the pan. Bake 20 mins. at 375.

COFFEE CAKE (Kaffee Kuchen)

For the Sponge:

- **½ cake yeast**
- **¼ cup lukewarm water**
- **1 cup milk**
- **½ teaspoon salt**
- **2 cups sifted flour**

At night crumble and soak yeast 20 minutes in lukewarm water. Scald milk, add salt and let cool. Add yeast to lukewarm milk and mix enough flour to make a thick batter. Beat smooth. Cover and let rise in moderately warm place (78 degrees) over night or until light.

For the Dough:

- **½ cup milk**
- **½ cup butter**
- **¾ cup sugar**
- **1 teaspoon salt**
- **2 eggs**
- **4 cups flour**

In morning scald and cool milk. Cream butter, sugar and salt. Add beaten eggs. Mix sponge with lukewarm milk, then add butter mixture and enough flour to make soft dough. Beat hard or knead by hand. Let dough rise until doubled. When light turn on floured board and roll out gently until ½ inch thick. Place in buttered pans. Brush top with melted butter. Let rise until double. Sprinkle with sugar or cinnamon and bake in hot oven for 20 minutes.

PENNSYLVANIA DUTCH

Cakes

SPONGE CAKE

- **3 eggs**
- **1 cup sugar**
- **1 cup flour**
- **½ tsp. salt**
- **1 tsp. baking powder**
- **3 tblsp. warm water**
- **1 tsp. lemon juice**

Beat the eggs until thick and creamy. Add sifted sugar and beat well. Add water and lemon juice and beat again. Sift the flour, add salt and baking powder and sift again. Combine dry ingredients with the egg mixture, a little at a time folding in gently. When well blended pour into an ungreased pan with center tube. Bake in moderate oven (350-f) for 50 minutes.

SCRIPTURE CAKE

Behold there was a cake baken. I-Kings, 9:16

- **½ cup butter**
  Judges, 5:25
- **2 cups flour**
  I-Kings, 4:22
- **½ tsp. salt**
  Leviticus, 2:13
- **1 cup figs**
  I-Samuel, 30:12
- **1½ cups sugar**
  Jeremiah, 6:20

- **2 tsp. baking powder**
  Luke, 13:21
- **½ cup water**
  Genesis, 24:11
- **1 cup raisins**
  I-Samuel, 30:12
- **3 eggs**
  Isaiah, 10:14
- **Cinnamon, mace, cloves**
  I-Kings, 10:10
- **1 tblsp. honey**
  Proverbs, 24:13
- **½ cup almonds**
  Genesis, 43:11

Blend butter, sugar, spices and salt. Beat egg yolks and add. Sift in baking powder and flour, then add the water and honey. Put fruit and nuts thru food chopper and flour well. Follow Solomon's advice for making good boys—1st clause of Proverbs, 23:14. Fold in stiffly beaten egg whites. Bake for 1 hour in 375-f oven.

SPICE LAYER CAKE

- **2 cups light brown sugar**
- **½ cup shortening**
- **2 eggs**
- **¾ cup milk**
- **3 tsp. baking powder**
- **1 cup chopped raisins**
- **2¼ cups flour**
- **1 tsp. cinnamon**
- **½ tsp. cloves**
- **½ tsp. nutmeg**
- **½ tsp. salt**

Cream sugar and shortening and beat until fluffy. Add the eggs and beat until light. Sift the flour, add salt, spices, baking powder, then sift again. Add the dry ingredients to the egg mixture alternately with the milk. Beat thoroughly and add the floured raisins. Pour into 2 greased layer cake pans. Bake in moderate oven (350-f) for 25 or 30 minutes. For the icing use:

- **2 cups sugar**
- **¾ cup milk**
- **2 tblsp. butter**

Cream together and boil until it forms a soft ball when dropped in water. Add vanilla and beat until cold. Spread between layers, over top and sides.

GRANDMOTHER'S MOLASSES CAKE

- **1 cup shortening**
- **1 cup sugar**
- **1 cup molasses**
- **1 teaspoon salt**
- **2 eggs**
- **1 cup raisins and currants**
- **flour to make a soft batter**
- **1 tablespoon ginger**
- **1 tablespoon cloves**
- **1 tablespoon cinnamon**
- **2 cups sour milk**
- **1 teaspoon baking soda**

Cream shortening and sugar. Add molasses and beaten eggs. Sift dry ingredients and add alternately with 1½ cups of sour milk. Mix the soda in the remaining milk and add with remainder of flour. Floured currants and raisins are added last. Bake in a loaf pan in a slow oven about one hour.

WALNUT GINGERBREAD

- **1 cup light brown sugar**
- **½ cup shortening**
- **½ cup black molasses**
- **1 cup boiling water**
- **3½ cups flour**
- **2 tsp. baking soda**
- **½ tsp. ginger**
- **½ tsp. cinnamon**
- **½ tsp. cloves**
- **2 eggs**
- **¾ cup chopped black walnuts**

Cream the sugar and shortening in a bowl. Add the molasses and pour the cup of boiling water over it. Mix well. Combine the flour, soda and spices, sift and add to the molasses mixture, beating well. Add the eggs one at a time and blend thoroughly. Next add the chopped nut meats. Pour into a well greased loaf pan and bake in moderate oven (350-f) for 40 minutes.

APPLE SAUCE CAKE

- **1 cup light brown sugar**
- **¼ cup butter**
- **1 cup apple sauce**
- **1 tsp. soda**
- **2 cups flour**
- **1 tsp. cinnamon**
- **½ tsp. cloves, ground**
- **a little nutmeg**
- **1 cup raisins**
- **pinch of salt**

Cream together butter, sugar and spices. Add apple sauce, flour and soda dissolved in a little warm water. Add the raisins (or currants). Beat thoroughly and pour into a loaf tin. Bake in moderate oven (350-f) for approximately 50 minutes.

ICING

1 cup pulverized sugar, piece of butter size of a walnut. Moisten with a little water and spread over cake.

NUT CAKE

- **1½ cups sugar**
- **½ cup butter**
- **3 eggs, separated**
- **2½ cups flour**
- **1 cup nut meats, chopped**
- **2 tsp. baking powder**
- **¾ cup milk**
- **a little salt**

Rub butter and sugar to a light, white cream. Add egg yolks and beat until smooth. Sift flour, salt and baking powder and add, together with milk, a little at a time, beating well. Fold in chopped nuts and stiffly beaten egg whites. Pour into 2 nine inch cake pans or 1 loaf pan. Bake in medium oven (350-f) for 30 minutes for layer cake or 1 hour for loaf cake. Use hickory nuts, black walnuts or shellbarks.

PENNSYLVANIA DUTCH

Cookies

ANISE COOKIES

- **6 eggs, separated**
- **1 cup powdered sugar**
- **1 cup flour, sifted**
- **3 tsps. anise seed**

Beat egg yolks until thick and foamy. Beat egg whites stiff and combine with egg yolks. Gradually add the powdered sugar and mix lightly. Sift flour and add to the egg mixture together with the anise seed. Drop from teaspoon on greased cookie sheet, spacing about 1 inch apart. Chill in refrigerator over night. Bake in slow oven (300-f) for about 12 minutes.

FRUIT *AND* NUT COOKIES

- **1 cup shortening**
- **1½ cups sugar**
- **3 eggs**
- **3½ cups flour**
- **1 tsp. salt**
- **1 tsp. cinnamon**
- **1 tsp. soda**
- **1½ tblsp. hot water**
- **½ cup raisins, chopped**
- **½ cup currants, chopped**
- **1 cup nuts, chopped**

Cream shortening and sugar, add the eggs and beat until light and fluffy. Sift flour add salt and cinnamon and sift again. Dissolve the soda in the hot water and add to the creamed mixture. Add half of the sifted dry ingredients mixing well. Fold in the chopped fruit and nuts and the remaining flour mixture. Stir until thoroughly blended. Drop teaspoonfuls on greased cookie sheets, about 2 inches apart and bake in moderate oven (350-f) for 15 minutes.

CINNAMON WAFFLES (Zimmet waffles)

- **½ lb. butter**
- **1 cup sugar**
- **2 tsp. cinnamon**
- **3 eggs**
- **flour**

Cream the butter and sugar. Beat in the eggs 1 at a time and add cinnamon. Work in enough flour to make a soft dough. Form into small balls. Place several in a hot waffle iron, suitably spaced, press down top and bake. This is an old recipe which the "dutch" brought over from Germany.

MORAVIAN CHRISTMAS COOKIES

- **½ cup shortening**
- **1 cup brown sugar**
- **1 cup molasses**
- **1 egg**
- **4 cups flour**
- **1 teaspoon cinnamon**
- **1 teaspoon cloves**
- **½ teaspoon nutmeg**
- **1 teaspoon soda**

Blend shortening, sugar and molasses. Add beaten egg. Sift dry ingredients and combine. Mix well, roll out and cut in fancy shapes. Bake at 350 degrees for 10 minutes. When cool decorate with boiled icing.

DUTCH ALMOND COOKIES

- **1 cup shortening**
- **½ cup white sugar**
- **1 cup brown sugar**
- **2 eggs**

- **½ teaspoon vanilla**
- **3 cups flour**
- **¼ teaspoon cinnamon**
- **¼ teaspoon nutmeg**
- **¼ teaspoon soda**
- **¼ teaspoon salt**
- **½ cup ground blanched almonds**

Cream shortening with white and brown sugar. Add 2 eggs and work in the sifted dry ingredients. Then add the chopped blanched almonds. Shape dough into long rolls. Roll in wax paper and store in cold place for 12 hours. Slice thin and bake in hot oven.

SAND TARTS

- **2 cups sugar**
- **1 cup butter**
- **4 eggs**
- **flour**

Work butter and part of the sugar together, then the remainder of the sugar and the eggs should be mixed in. Use flour enough to make very stiff. Roll thin, cut out in small squares, wet top with two eggs beaten, sprinkle with sugar, cinnamon and chopped almonds. Bake in moderate oven, 10 minutes.

WALNUT KISSES

- **1 lb. sugar**
- **6 egg whites**
- **3 tablespoons flour**
- **2 cups walnuts chopped**

Beat egg whites until stiff and dry. Mix flour and sugar and fold in stiffly beaten egg whites. Add walnuts and bake in moderate oven, 375 degrees.

WALNUT ROCKS

- **1 cup butter**
- **1½ cups brown sugar**
- **3 eggs, beaten**
- **1 tsp. soda**
- **1½ tblsp. hot water**
- **3 cups flour**
- **½ tsp. salt**

- **1 tsp. cinnamon**
- **½ tsp. cloves**
- **1½ cups chopped raisins**
- **1 cup chopped walnuts**

Cream butter and sugar and add the beaten eggs. Dissolve soda in the hot water and add to the creamed mixture. Sift flour, salt and spices twice and add half of it to mixture and mix thoroughly. Combine chopped raisins and nuts with the other half and add to the dough. Mix thoroughly and drop by teaspoonfuls onto greased baking sheets spaced a couple of inches apart. Bake in moderate oven (350-f) for 12 to 15 minutes.

LEBKUCHEN

- **1½ cups flour**
- **1 tblsp. cinnamon**
- **½ tsp. nutmeg**
- **½ tsp. cloves, ground**
- **½ tsp. cream of tartar**
- **2 eggs, beaten**
- **1 cup dark brown sugar**
- **⅛ lb. citron, chopped fine**
- **⅛ lb. almonds, chopped**

Sift the flour, cinnamon, nutmeg, cloves and cream of tartar. Mix the sugar and beaten eggs thoroughly. Combine with the flour mixture, add citron and the almonds. Roll out on floured board, ¼ inch thick. Place on a greased cookie sheet and bake in moderate oven (350-f) for 15 minutes. Cut into squares or diamonds while still warm. Ice thinly with plain white or lemon frosting. This is an old recipe for an oldtime Christmas favorite.

CHRISTMAS BUTTER COOKIES

- **1 cup soft butter**
- **½ cup brown sugar, packed**
- **2¼ cups flour, sifted**

Cream butter until it resembles whipped cream and slowly add the sugar, beating well. Add flour gradually and blend thoroughly. Wrap in waxed paper and chill for several hours. Knead dough slightly on floured board, form into a smooth ball. Roll to about ⅛ inch thick and cut to desired shapes. Place on ungreased cookie sheets and bake in moderate oven (350-f) about 12 minutes. When cold decorate with butter icing, candied fruit, etc.

ALMOND MACAROONS

- **1 cup almond paste**
- **¾ cup sugar**
- **3 egg whites**
- **salt**

Rub paste until smooth, gradually work in the sugar until well mixed. Add a pinch of salt and beat in one egg white at a time, mixing thoroughly. Let stand for 20 minutes. Drop teaspoonfuls on lightly buttered baking sheet. Bake in slow oven (300-f) for 25 or 30 minutes until surface is dry. Keep in cool place overnight.

SUGAR CAKES

- **3 cups sugar**
- **¾ cup butter**
- **2 eggs**
- **2 teaspoons baking soda**
- **1 cup thick milk**

Mix eggs and butter well. Then add milk and soda. Mix in enough flour to make a soft dough, just so you can roll it. Cut into any shapes you wish. Sprinkle with granulated sugar, bake in a moderately heated oven.

HICKORY NUT KISSES

- **2 cups sugar**
- **2 cups hickory nuts, chopped fine**
- **6 egg whites**
- **3 tablespoons flour**

Beat egg whites lightly, add sugar, then nut kernels, lastly the flour. Drop on greased tins and bake in moderate oven. 350 degrees.

"BELSNICKEL" CHRISTMAS CAKES

- **1 cup sugar**
- **½ cup melted butter**
- **2 eggs**
- **1½ cups flour**
- **½ tsp. baking soda**
- **pinch of salt**

Pour melted butter over sugar in a bowl and beat until smooth and creamy. Add the eggs, beating one at a time, into the mixture. Sift the baking soda thru the flour add the salt and add to the cake mixture. Stand the dough in a cold place for an hour. Roll out on floured board, quite thin. Cut into small rounds or other shapes. Sprinkle with sugar and bake in hot oven (400-f) for 10 minutes.

GINGER COOKIES—GINGERBREAD MEN

- **⅔ cup shortening**
- **½ cup brown sugar**
- **2 tsp. ginger**
- **1 tsp. cinnamon**
- **¼ tsp. cloves or allspice**
- **1½ tsp. salt**
- **1 egg**
- **¾ cup molasses**
- **3 cups flour, sifted**
- **1 tsp. soda**
- **½ tsp. baking powder**

Cream together shortening, brown sugar, spices and salt. Add the egg, mix thoroughly. Add molasses and blend. Sift together twice the flour, soda, baking powder and add to the molasses mixture. Stir well and chill. Roll out a fourth of the dough at a time, on floured board to a little more than ⅛ inch thick. Cut with gingerbread man cutters or other shapes. Bake on greased cookie sheets in moderately hot (375-f) oven, 8 to 10 minutes. Cool before decorating.

PFEFFERNUSSE

- **3 eggs**
- **½ lb. powdered sugar**
- **2 cups flour**
- **½ tsp. cinnamon**

- **¼ tsp. cloves**
- **¼ tsp. nutmeg**
- **½ tsp. soda**
- **¼ tsp. salt**
- **1 lemon, juice and rind**

Beat eggs well, gradually add powdered sugar, lemon juice and grated rind. Sift flour and add salt, soda and spices. Sift again and add to egg and sugar mixture. Beat to form smooth, medium-soft dough. Chill in refrigerator for several hours. Roll out on floured board, into long finger-shaped sticks. Cut into small marble sized pieces and bake on greased baking sheets in hot oven (425-f) until they turn a light, golden brown.

MORAVIAN DARK COOKIES

- **½ lb. butter**
- **1 cup sugar**
- **1 tblsp. cream**
- **2 cups dark molasses**
- **1 tblsp. cinnamon**
- **½ tblsp. ginger**
- **½ tsp. cloves, ground**
- **8 cups flour**

Cream the butter and sugar together until smooth. Add the cream, molasses, cinnamon, ginger and cloves and blend smooth. Work in the flour gradually. Roll out as thin as possible on floured board. Cut into various shapes with cookie cutters. Bake on greased cookie sheets in moderate oven (350-f) for about 12 minutes. Decorate using a pastry tube and icing made from egg-white and confectioners sugar.

PENNSYLVANIA DUTCH

Pies

PUMPKIN PIE

- **1½ cups mashed cooked pumpkin**
- **1½ cups rich milk**
- **¾ cup brown sugar**
- **2 eggs**
- **pastry for 9" shell**
- **1 tsp. cinnamon**
- **½ tsp. ginger**
- **¼ tsp. cloves, powdered**
- **¾ tsp. salt**
- **2 tblsp. butter, melted**

Place all ingredients in a bowl and beat well with a rotary egg beater. Chill and pour into an unbaked pie shell. Bake in hot oven (450-f) for 10 minutes. Reduce heat to moderately slow oven (325-f). When surface of pie filling turns light brown, test by inserting a silver knife. If it comes out clean the pie is finished baking.

LEMON CUSTARD PIE

- **2 tablespoons flour**
- **½ cup sugar**
- **2 eggs, separated**
- **pinch of salt**
- **1 lemon**
- **1½ cups milk**
- **1 pie shell**

Mix 2 tablespoons of flour with ½ cup sugar and a pinch of salt. Beat 2 egg yolks. Add the juice and grated rind of 1 lemon. Then add flour and sugar continuing to beat. Stir in 1½ cups milk and lastly fold in 2 egg whites beaten stiff, but not dry. Pour into unbaked pie shell. Bake in hot oven, 425 degrees for 15 minutes. Reduce heat to moderate 350 degrees and bake 15 minutes more.

PENNSYLVANIA DUTCH SOUR CHERRY PIE

- **1 qt. fresh sour cherries**
- **1½ cups sugar**
- **½ cup flour**
- **pie crust**

Mix flour and sugar and pitted cherries in a bowl. Fill unbaked pie crust with the cherries. Put on a top pie crust, vented and bake in a hot oven for 10 minutes. Reduce to moderate and bake for 20 minutes more.

RIVEL (CRUMB) PIE

- **1 cup flour**
- **½ cup sugar**
- **½ cup butter and shortening mixed**

Mix or "crumb" the above ingredients together with the hands to form small lumps or rivels. Strew the rivels into a prepared pastry shell and bake in a hot oven (400-f) for 30 minutes. Some spread 2 tblsps. of molasses over it before baking.

SOUR CREAM RAISIN PIE

- **1 cup sugar**
- **¾ teaspoon cinnamon**
- **¼ teaspoon nutmeg**
- **⅛ teaspoon salt**
- **1 cup thick sour cream**
- **3 eggs, slightly beaten**
- **2 cups raisins, ground**
- **1 unbaked pie shell**

Combine all ingredients and turn into uncooked pie shell. Bake in hot, 450 degree oven 15 minutes, and then reduce to 350 degrees for 30 minutes.

CREAM RASPBERRY PIE

After lining a pie plate with pie crust, fill it with red raspberries. Cover it with granulated sugar and with an upper crust, but rub the edges of both upper and lower crusts with butter, so they will not stick together. Then when pie is baked make a cream filling with:

- **1 cup milk**
- **1 teaspoon cornstarch**
- **2 tablespoons sugar**
- **vanilla**

Cook this and when cool, add the whites of three eggs stiffly beaten. Lift the upper crust of the pie and pour in this cream filling. Replace the crust and sift with powdered sugar.

PASTRY HINT

When making a fruit pie, put lower crust in the oven 5 minutes and bake while you are rolling out the top crust. Then put in filling and put on the top crust. The undercrust will not be soggy.

MONTGOMERY PIE

For the syrup part:

- **½ cup molasses**
- **½ cup sugar**

- **1 egg**
- **1 cup water**
- **2 tblsp. flour**
- **½ lemon, juice and rind**

Combine above ingredients and pour into a 9 inch, unbaked pie shell.

For the topping:

- **⅔ cup sugar**
- **¼ cup butter**
- **1 egg, beaten**
- **1 tsp. baking powder**
- **1 cup milk**
- **1½ cups flour**

Blend butter and sugar, add egg and beat well. Add milk and the sifted dry ingredients a little at a time. Spread topping over mixture in the pie shell. Bake in moderate oven (350-f) for 40 minutes.

APPLE CRUMB PIE

- **6 tart apples**
- **1 cup sugar**
- **⅓ cup butter**
- **¾ cup flour**
- **1 tsp. cinnamon**
- **pastry for 9" shell**

Pare apples and cut into thick slices. Mix half the sugar with the cinnamon and sprinkle over apples. Put into unbaked pastry shell. Blend the flour, the remaining sugar and the butter and work into small crumbs, with your fingers. Sprinkle the crumbs over the apples. Bake in hot oven (425-f) for 10 minutes then reduce to moderate (350-f) and bake for 35 minutes more. Serve with cheese.

BLACK WALNUT PIE

- **4 eggs**
- **3 tablespoons flour**
- **1½ cups sugar**
- **1 cup black walnuts, chopped**
- **1½ cups water**
- **1¼ cups dark corn syrup**

Make crust for 2 pies and line medium size pie plates. Sprinkle the walnuts over the crusts and then mix in the filling. The eggs must be well beaten before adding the sugar gradually. Then fold in flour, corn syrup and 1½ cups of water. Bake in very hot oven for three minutes and then reduce to medium for 30 or 40 minutes.

FUNERAL PIE

- **1 cup seeded raisins, washed**
- **2 cups water**
- **1½ cups sugar**
- **4 tablespoons flour**
- **1 egg, well beaten**
- **juice of a lemon**
- **2 teaspoons grated lemon rind**
- **pinch of salt**

Soak raisins 3 hours, mix sugar, flour and egg. Then add seasoning, raisins and liquid. Cook over hot water for 15 minutes, stirring occasionally. When the mixture is cool, empty into pie-dough lined pie plate. Cover pie with narrow strips of dough, criss-crossed and bake until browned.

COTTAGE CHEESE PIE

- **1½ cups cottage cheese**
- **½ cup sugar**
- **2 tblsp. flour**
- **¼ tsp. salt**
- **2 eggs, separated**
- **2 cups milk**
- **¼ tsp. cinnamon**
- **½ tsp. lemon rind grated**
- **pie crust**

Combine cottage cheese, sugar, flour, salt, lemon rind and spices. Add beaten egg yolks and mix thoroughly. Add milk gradually and stir smooth. Fold in beaten egg whites and pour into 9 inch, pastry lined pan. Bake in moderate (350-f) oven, 1 hour.

APPLE BUTTER PIE

- **½ cup apple butter**
- **2 eggs**
- **½ cup sugar**
- **1½ tblsp. cornstarch**
- **1 tsp. cinnamon**
- **2 cups milk**
- **Pastry for 9 inch crust and strips for top**

Combine apple butter, beaten eggs, sugar, cornstarch and cinnamon and mix well. Add the milk gradually to the mixture and blend well. Pour into unbaked pie shell. Top with "lattice" made from ½ inch wide strips of crust. Bake at 350-f, 35 minutes.

CURRANT *AND* RED RASPBERRY PIE

Fill an unbaked pie shell with currants and red raspberries. Sugar generously. Add the top crust and bake for 30 minutes. This is unusual and very delicious.

SCHNITZ PIE (Dried apples)

- **1 lb. of schnitz**
- **1 orange, rind and juice**
- **2 cups sugar**
- **2 tblsp. cinnamon**
- **prepared pie crust**

Cover Schnitz with water and soak over night. Add orange rind and juice and more water if necessary. Boil until soft, then put through colander and add sugar and cinnamon. Pour into pastry lined shell, dot with butter, cover with top crust or lattice strips. Bake in hot oven (450-f) for 10 minutes. Reduce to 350-f bake 30 minutes.

RHUBARB PIE

- **3 cups diced rhubarb**
- **1½ cups sugar**
- **3 tblsp. flour**
- **¼ tsp. salt**
- **1 tblsp. lemon juice**
- **2 eggs, separated**
- **1 9-inch pie shell**

Cut rhubarb into small pieces and arrange in an unbaked pie shell. Combine the sugar and flour, add egg yolks and lemon juice. Stir into a smooth paste. Pour this mixture over rhubarb. Cover with meringue made from the egg white. Bake in a hot oven (425-f) for 10 minutes, then reduce heat to (325-f) and bake for 30 minutes.

PENNSYLVANIA DUTCH

Desserts

STEAMED FRUIT PUDDING

- **1 cup raisins**
- **1 cup chopped suet**
- **1 cup molasses**
- **1 cup milk**
- **1 tsp. salt**
- **1 tsp. soda**
- **¼ cup boiling water**
- **½ tsp. cinnamon**
- **½ tsp. nutmeg**
- **½ tsp. allspice**
- **½ tsp. cloves**
- **flour**

Combine and mix all the ingredients with flour enough to make a stiff batter; then add the soda dissolved in boiling water. Put into a well greased mould, cover tightly and steam for 3 hours. Serve with a sauce made from:

- **1 cup brown sugar**
- **1 tsp. vanilla**
- **1 egg, beaten**

Beat all together until creamy and pour over the pudding when serving.

APPLE *OR* PEACH STRUDEL

Into bottom of a buttered baking dish put thick layers of apples (or peaches). Sprinkle with sugar and cinnamon mixed. Dot with lumps of butter. Into a mixing bowl sift:

- **1 cup sugar**
- **1 tsp. baking powder**
- **1 cup flour**
- **½ tsp. salt**

Into this break 1 egg. Mix until crumbly. Put over apples (peaches) bake in moderate oven (350-f) till crust is brown. Serve with milk, whipped cream or ice cream.

COTTAGE PUDDING

- **1¾ cups flour**
- **2½ tsp. baking powder**
- **½ tsp. salt**
- **¼ cup butter, or other fat**
- **¾ cup sugar**
- **1 egg**
- **½ tsp. lemon extract**
- **⅔ cup milk**

Mix flour, baking powder and salt and sift twice. Cream butter until soft; add sugar gradually, beating until light. Beat in the egg and flavoring. Add flour mixing alternately with the milk, beating smooth after each addition. Turn into a buttered square tin (8 × 8 × 2 inches). Bake in moderate oven (350-f) for about 40 minutes. Serve with butterscotch or orange sauce. It's delicious covered with crushed berries or other fruits.

RHUBARB PUDDING

- **Stewed Rhubarb**
- **Stale cake or bread**
- **Sugar**
- **Whites of 2 eggs**

Line buttered baking dish with slices of plain stale cake or bread. Fill with sweetened rhubarb. Cover and bake in moderately slow oven (325-f) for 30 minutes. Make a meringue by beating egg whites stiff and adding 4 tblsp. sugar. Remove pudding from oven, cover with meringue and brown in oven.

CHERRY PUDDING

- **½ cup sugar**
- **¼ cup butter**
- **2 tsp. baking powder**
- **2½ cups flour**
- **1 cup milk**
- **1 cup cherries, pitted**
- **1 egg**

Cream together the butter and sugar and add the egg then beat well. Sift the flour and baking powder and add alternately with the milk. Blend well, flour the cherries and stir in. Pour batter into a baking dish and bake in moderate oven (350-f) for 30 mins. Serve with plain or whipped cream.

APPLE PANDOWDY

- **4 tart apples**
- **½ cup molasses**
- **½ teaspoon cinnamon**
- **2 tablespoons butter**
- **biscuit dough**

Pare and slice apples and arrange in a well greased shallow baking dish. Sprinkle with cinnamon, drizzle over molasses and dot with butter. Cover with biscuit dough which has been rolled to about ½ inch thickness. Cut gashes in dough to allow steam to escape. Bake in moderate oven about 375 degrees for 30 minutes. Serve hot, cutting out squares of the biscuit to use as a base for the fruit mixture. Serve with cream flavored with nutmeg.

APPLE DUMPLINGS

- **rich baking powder**
- **biscuit dough**
- **6 apples, medium size**
- **½ cup brown sugar**
- **½ teaspoon salt**
- **1 teaspoon cinnamon**
- **1 teaspoon nutmeg**
- **½ cup raisins**
- **2 tablespoons butter**

Prepare biscuit dough, roll ¼ inch thick and cut into squares. Pare and core apples and place one in center of each square. Fill each with a portion of the seasonings, sugar, raisins and dot with butter. Bring corners of the dough to the top of the apples and seal by pricking with a fork. Bake at 375 degrees for 30 minutes. Serve with cream or milk.

PUMPKIN CUSTARD

- **2 cups pumpkin, sieved**
- **1 cup soft bread crumbs**
- **2 eggs, separated**
- **1½ cups milk**
- **1 cup sugar**
- **3 tblsps. butter, melted**
- **¼ tsp. salt**
- **1 tsp. orange flavoring**

Combine ingredients except egg whites in the order listed and mix well after each addition. Pour into baking dish or custard cups. Bake in a slow oven (325-f) until mixture thickens and browns. Beat the egg whites, adding 2 tablespoons of sugar, until stiff, spread on top of custard and brown lightly.

PEACH DUMPLINGS

- **1 cup sugar**
- **1 tablespoon butter**
- **1 cup milk or cream**
- **2 cups sliced peaches**
- **1 cup flour**
- **2 teaspoons baking powder**
- **½ teaspoon salt**
- **2 cups hot water**

Make a syrup of the sugar with the butter and 2 cups hot water. Add the peaches. Let this come to a boil. Make dumplings by mixing flour and baking powder and salt into a fairly stiff batter with milk or cream. Drop large spoonfuls of this batter into the boiling syrup and peaches. Cover and cook for 20 minutes. Serve while hot.

Sweets and Sours

MIXED FRUIT PRESERVES

- **3 cups sour cherries**
- **3 cups fresh apricots**
- **2 cups red raspberries**
- **7 cups sugar**

Wash and seed cherries. Drop the apricots into boiling water for a few seconds, remove skins and seeds. Cut into quarters. Wash the berries. Mix the fruit and sugar together and cook quickly, until fruits are clear and tender. Seal in hot jars.

BREAD *AND* BUTTER PICKLES

- **1 gal. cucumbers**
- **8 onions**
- **½ cup salt**
- **2 green peppers**
- **2 red peppers**

Slice cucumbers, onions and peppers. Pack in ice. Let stand 3 hours. Put a heavy weight on top the pickles. A plate with a weight on top is best. Drain well and combine with:

- **5 cups sugar**
- **2 tablespoons mustard seed**
- **2 tablespoons celery seed**
- **1½ teaspoons turmeric**
- **½ teaspoon ground cloves**
- **5 cups vinegar**

Mix well. Pour over pickles and simmer 30 minutes. Seal in hot jars.

RASPBERRY RHUBARB JAM

- **3 lbs. rhubarb**
- **2½ cups sugar**
- **½ cup water**

- **2 oranges, juice and rind**
- **2 cups raspberries**

Skin and cut rhubarb into ½ inch pieces. Add water and sugar, the orange juice and grated peel. Cook all together, stirring frequently to prevent scorching, for 30 minutes, or until clear. Put in sterile jelly glasses and seal.

CARROT MARMALADE

- **1 lb. carrots**
- **1½ lbs. sugar**
- **2 lemons**
- **½ cup chopped nuts**

Clean and scrape carrots, cook until soft, then mash. Add sugar, juice of 2 lemons and the grated rind of 1 lemon. Cook 20 minutes, stirring frequently. Add the chopped nuts, pour into hot, sterile jars and seal.

APPLE *AND* PEACH CONSERVE

- **2 cups apples, chopped**
- **2 cups peaches, chopped**
- **juice of 2 lemons**
- **3 cups sugar**

Use tart unpeeled apples and firm ripe peaches, cut into small pieces. Combine with lemon juice and sugar. Cook slowly until the apple is transparent (about 20 minutes). Pour into sterilized glasses, seal. Makes 7 6-oz. glasses.

SPICED GOOSEBERRIES

- **5 lbs. ripe gooseberries**
- **4 lbs. brown sugar**
- **2 cups vinegar**
- **2 tblsps. cloves**
- **3 tsps. cinnamon**
- **3 tsps. allspice**

Wash and pick over gooseberries. Combine with sugar, vinegar, spices and cook slowly until mixture becomes rather thick. Pour into sterilized glasses and seal. 5 pints.

CRANBERRY CONSERVE

- **4 cups cranberries**
- **2 large oranges**
- **1 cup chopped raisins**
- **2 cups hot water**
- **4 cups sugar**
- **1 cup chopped nuts**

Cut oranges into quarters and remove seeds. Grind cranberries and oranges, fruit and rind in food chopper. Add the hot water and bring to a boil. Cook quickly until fruit is soft. Add sugar and raisins. Cook over moderate heat, stirring often, until thickened. Add chopped walnuts or blanched almonds.

APPLE BUTTER

- **4 qts. apples**
- **2 qts. apple cider**
- **2 cups sugar**
- **2 cups dark corn syrup**
- **1 tsp. cinnamon**

Boil the cider until reduced to 1 quart. Pare the apples and slice thin. Put the apples into the cider and cook very slowly, stirring frequently, until it begins to thicken. Add sugar, syrup and cinnamon and continue to cook until thick enough to spread when cool. Seal in sterilized jars. Makes 5 to 6 pints.

SPICED CANTALOUPE

- **3 lbs. cantaloupe**
- **½ tblsp. alum**
- **2 qts. water**
- **3 cups sugar**
- **1 pt. vinegar**
- **2 sticks cinnamon**
- **½ tblsp. whole cloves**
- **1 tsp. allspice**

Pare the cantaloupe, remove seeds and cut into strips, 1 × 2 inch or squares. Dissolve the alum in the water and bring to a boil. Add the cantaloupe and cook for 15 minutes. Drain well. Combine vinegar, sugar and spices. Add the cantaloupe and simmer slowly until fruit is transparent (about 45 minutes). Place in hot sterilized jars and seal.

RED BEET EGGS

When making pickled beets, save some of the spicy pickling liquid and put into it a half-dozen, shelled, hard-boiled eggs. These take on a beautiful color and excellent flavor and are grand as appetizers served with crisp hearts of celery. They are also good sliced in sandwiches or salads.

GINGER PEARS

- **5 lbs. hard pears**
- **3 cups water**
- **5 lbs. sugar**
- **½ cup chopped preserved ginger**
- **3 lemons juice and rind**

Pare and core the pears. Dice or cut into thin slices. Add water and cook until tender. Add the sugar, ginger, the lemon juice and grated rind. Simmer mixture until thick and pears are transparent. Pour into sterilized jars and seal. Makes 5 pints.

PICKLED BEETS

- **3 lbs. beets**
- **1 stick cinnamon**
- **1 teaspoon whole allspice**
- **½ cup sugar**
- **6 whole cloves**
- **1 pt. vinegar**
- **½ cup water**

Boil beets until tender. Remove skins. Tie spices in cheesecloth. Heat vinegar, water, sugar and spices to boiling point. Add beets and boil 5 minutes. Pack in sterile jars and fill with hot liquid. Seal.

CORN RELISH

- **9 ears corn**

- **1 qt. vinegar**
- **1 cup sugar**
- **1 tsp. salt**
- **1½ tblsps. dry mustard**
- **1 tsp. turmeric**
- **1 medium head cabbage**
- **2 medium onions, chopped**
- **3 red peppers**
- **2 green peppers**

Cook corn in boiling water for 2 minutes. Dip in cold water and cut grains from the cob. Chop the cabbage, onion and peppers into small pieces and add to corn. Mix vinegar, sugar, salt and spices and heat to boiling. Add the corn and vegetables and boil until tender, 20 to 30 minutes, stirring frequently. Pour into sterile jars and seal. This makes about 8 pints.

PEPPER RELISH

- **12 sweet red peppers**
- **12 sweet green peppers**
- **8 small onions**
- **1 qt. vinegar**
- **1½ cups sugar**
- **2 tsp. salt**

Seed the peppers and chop fine with the onion. Put into a bowl, cover with boiling water and let stand for 5 minutes. Drain and cover again with boiling water, let stand for 10 minutes longer. Place in colander or cheesecloth bag let drain over night. In the morning add the vinegar, sugar and salt. Boil for 20 minutes. Place in hot sterilized jars and seal.

PICKLED GREEN BEANS

- **2 cups green beans**
- **1 cup vinegar**
- **1 cup sugar**
- **1 cup water**

Clean and cook whole green beans. Place them in a sterile pint jar. Boil the water, vinegar, sugar and ⅛ tsp. salt. Pour over the beans and seal jar.

CHOW CHOW

- **2 qts. chopped cabbage**
- **1 qt. chopped green tomatoes**
- **6 large onions, chopped**
- **3 sweet red peppers, chopped**
- **salt**
- **2 lbs. sugar**
- **4 tablespoons dry mustard**
- **3 tblsp. white mustard seed**
- **1½ tablespoons celery seed**
- **½ tablespoon ginger**
- **vinegar to cover (about 8 cups)**
- **1 tablespoon cloves**

Put each kind of vegetable into a separate bowl and sprinkle a small amount of salt over each. Let stand 4 hours. Press juice from each vegetable and combine. Mix the dry ingredients and rub into a paste by using a small amount of vinegar. Then add all the vinegar and heat to boiling. Put in the vegetables and cook slowly for 20 minutes. Pack in sterile jars and seal. Cover jars with boiling water and simmer for 15 minutes. Makes 2½ quarts.

CPSIA information can be obtained
at www.ICGtesting.com
Printed in the USA
LVHW061948191222
735554LV00011B/411

9 781805 470755